FORWARD THINKING

FOR YOUR

BUSINESS

It's not who you know in business,
it's who knows you.

Jennifer Layman

Global Book
Publishing

Forward Thinking for Your Business
Jennifer Layman
©2023 Jennifer Layman. All rights reserved.

ISBN: 978-1-956193-49-7
Book Design & Publishing done by:
Global Book Publishing
www.globalbookpublishing.com

To every person who had the courage to start their own business and to the people who supported them. I love you Mom and Dad.

Table of Contents

How You Can Use This Book

Many business owners don't have a lot of time for marketing. People are busy, and time is limited. Things that are not immediately necessary can be deferred, and marketing is often in that category. And then one day, you hear your competitor's ad on the radio or see they have acquired a company and are expanding their services. You feel the need to do something to remind customers you're still here, so you scramble to buy some ads.

Suddenly, you are reacting to what your competitor is doing.

The problem with reacting is that you are just playing catch-up. You are always behind your competitors, chasing them, not leading. When you're the leader, you have more opportunities to gain customers, ward off competition, and take your business to the level you want to take it. Marketing can help achieve that.

You can make better marketing decisions by focusing on certain things and thinking in a certain way. This is not about spending more time on marketing but about spending the time you do have in a more effective way.

Having worked with a varying clientele of business owners, from single owner-operators to multi-million-dollar organizations, there are common situations that prevent businesses from marketing effectively. Foremost among them is time. If I am going to convince you to use marketing to your advantage, I must be efficient with your time or else it won't get done. I get that; it's why the chapters in this book are short and on point.

Business owners have a truly unique drive and determination. Businesses provide products and services to communities, which influences community growth and prosperity. Business owners are experts in what they do, but they are not always experts in marketing what they do.

If you are going to reach your potential in your business, you must make good marketing decisions. To make good marketing decisions, you need some insight into what is worth pursuing and what won't bring you the expected value. The impact of marketing decisions is not immediate; it happens over time, so if you are pursuing the wrong thing, you won't know that right away. What you need is a quick reference, a guide of sorts, on how to make the best decisions.

To make the best decisions, you need to know two things: what to do and how to do it. This book is your reference to accomplish that.

1

What Marketing Is and Why It Matters

It is difficult to be motivated to do something when you don't understand what it is and why it matters.

Marketing is everything you do to make people aware of your business. Most of the time, we think of marketing as being promotional in nature: advertising, business cards, in-store sales, or customer appreciation events. But marketing is also evident in how you sell your business—conveying product information, putting together a proposal for a contract, and the customer service you offer when someone makes a call or sends an email to ask about a product or service you provide. Every time you communicate with someone, whether indirectly through advertising or directly through a phone call, you are marketing your business.

If you think about how often you communicate with a current or potential customer, you will soon realize you are marketing every day. It is perhaps the one thing you do more than anything else in your business, so it matters a great deal that you do it well.

This book contains specific aspects of marketing that guide you to making the best presentation of your business in the most effective manner. I also want to address some of the frustrations that business owners face with marketing and provide you with some ways to think about marketing that give you greater control (and less stress) to do it well.

Here are some things I have heard people say when they are resistant to investing in marketing.

I Did Marketing Before, But it Didn't Work

Marketing involves three things: saying the right thing to the right people at the right time. If your past marketing efforts didn't work, one of these things was off. This book will discuss how to say the right things, choose the right people to hear it, and select the best time to prompt action.

I Have a Hard Time Seeing Results from Marketing

You must give yourself some time for marketing to build. There is a chapter in this book where you can complete a one-page marketing plan to help guide you through a year of decision-making. Marketing is a continual process, and when you have a guide on what you plan to do, it will make the time you spend on marketing more efficient and productive.

I Don't Have Time to Do Marketing

Only a business owner understands how much time goes into running your business. I totally get that, because I run my own small business, and I must make time for all sorts of things: government remittances, handling customer inquiries, invoicing, etc. Marketing is something you need to make time for, and when you know what to do, it is easier to make the time to do it. This book will help you know what to do so you can make the time to do it.

I Have Been Here for Years, and People Still Say They Didn't Know About Me! How Can That Be?

First of all, congratulations for being the owner of a long-standing business. Second, it is important to recognize that while your business may have been in the same place for twenty years, your customers have not! As people age, their needs become different. When I was twenty-five, I didn't have a home, so I didn't need plumbing services, roof repair, flooring, furniture, etc. I didn't respond to marketing on those things. But fifteen years later, I bought a house, and now I do need all those things. As people's lives change, so do their needs. That's why you must keep marketing.

Word Of Mouth Is the Best Advertising

Nothing is better than having someone rave about your business, but that doesn't mean they will drive business your way. For example, I remember recommending an HVAC business to someone, and they replied with, *"Yes, I called them, but they couldn't come for a week, so I'm looking for someone else."* Good word of mouth, but it didn't result in a sale. It is always a stronger position to communicate your business yourself than to rely on others to do it for you. Word of mouth is like icing on the cake, but you still must provide the cake!

If you think more people should be your customers, you're probably right. By doing certain things in a certain way, you can make that happen. You must plan ahead a little, like you would when making a dentist appointment or a dinner reservation, and once you decide to do it, you will make your own results. You have gotten this far because you are interested in how marketing can build your business. Now, let's get committed to doing it.

2

We've Been Here for Years

When we don't want to do something, we can find 'reasons' to justify that position. When businesses don't want to put money into marketing, they sometimes find similar reasons. One of my favourites is, *"We don't have to do marketing. We've been here for years. Everyone knows us."*

These are the same business owners who complain that people aren't as loyal as they used to be, that the internet has ruined everything or that we are in a recession—a cause beyond their control. While those things can be true, what can also be true is that business is slow because you stopped communicating with people.

The *'everyone knows us'* defence is a shortcut to closure. First, even if you are right and everyone who could ever be your customer knows everything that you offer, it doesn't mean they will spend their time or money with you.

The criteria for having a customer is beyond just knowing someone.

Second, it is likely everyone *doesn't* know you. While you may have been in the community for fifty or even one hundred years, it is not likely everyone else has been. Residential populations do not stay the same in communities, even slower-changing communities. If someone moves from one end of town to the other, they can literally change their buying habits. And not to mention that people are born every single day. The population certainly changes, even if you don't.

Third, if you rely on word of mouth to attract customers, it only works if a) you make it into the conversation, and b) you're not trumped by a better option. Here's an example: *Store A and Store B are really great stores, but Store B is open longer.* Both stores earned positive word of mouth, yet Store A still loses the customer.

If none of this convinces you, here is one final way to consider the '*everyone knows us*' line of defence.

Years ago, we had fewer options to choose from, especially in rural areas. If you sold shoes, you were probably known as '*the shoe store*' more than your proper name. It was like eating at a buffet with only one choice.

As more shoe-selling stores opened, people had more choices—or more options at the buffet table, and they tried some new things. They may still like your store, but perhaps another store had a better colour selection or a sale or was open longer and, thus, more accessible.

14

And then came the internet, and choice took on a whole new meaning. Instead of attending workshops, you can listen to a webinar. Instead of browsing through a physical store, you can browse an online store. The buffet basically became a visual overload for people in choices. Today's sale is about the customer getting what they want, not the customer choosing from what you have.

The moral of this story is that it is never time to rest on your laurels. If you have been successful in the community for fifty years, keep that going! Change the things that need changing and keep communicating with people. You deserve it.

3

Word of Mouth vs. Referrals

It feels great to gain a new customer because a current customer referred you to them. For some businesses, referrals are a big part of what drives people through their front doors. I have worked with lawyers who derive more than 80 percent of their clientele through referrals, which is critical information when it comes to working on a marketing strategy. You might wonder why a lawyer would even need to spend time on marketing when they could live off referred business. The reason is because it ensures they are always in control of how people perceive their business.

Cause and Effect

In any given situation, you are either at cause or at effect for the outcomes of your business. When you are at cause, it means you have the ability to impact your results, so you are doing things to make those results happen. When you are at effect, it means you are justifying why things are happening to your business. Circumstances are beyond your control and you're just reacting. You can easily see why the more powerful position is to be actively involved in influencing your results.

When you are marketing, you are sending a certain message about your business. People see it based on where you decide to promote it. You are causing them to remember it based on the frequency with which you communicate it. When you are marketing, you are actively involved in driving results in your business.

Referrals are something that put you at effect in your business. You cannot control the referral, but you can react to it, accept it, and use it as a great start to building a relationship with your new customer. Referrals are good effects. Positive word of mouth is also a good effect. You just don't have any control over them. So, if your marketing strategy is based on things you cannot control, you are also relinquishing control of your results. Why not benefit from both?

Keep active with your marketing to build awareness from people who could be your customer, but do not know someone who knows you. Trust me, there are a lot of those people, and any one of them could become one of your best customers, so they are worth the effort. The other thing marketing can do for you is to be an alternative voice to any negative word of mouth. If someone speaks negatively about your business, your marketing messages can help counteract that situation for the customer and maybe influence them to give you a call anyway. If the only message someone hears about your business is negative word of mouth, it is unlikely the customer will still seek you out.

It is important to know that negative word of mouth is not always directed to your business. Consider this:

> Sally: I'm thinking about buying a bicycle. Didn't you get yours from ABC Company?
>
> Anne: I did, and they were good to deal with, but have you been to the new bicycle store that just opened? They might be worth checking out first. I haven't been there yet, so I'll go with you if you want.

Both women had positive word of mouth for the bicycle shop, and one even made a purchase there, but they went somewhere else anyway.

Some Other Considerations

1. People who know your business don't always remain in the community. A new job can take them to another city. So can retirement. So can marriages and divorces, expanding families, and empty nest situations. When people move, they take their referrals with them.

2. In businesses and organizations, employee changes can also impact referral opportunities. When those key people retire or move on, business referrals can change.

3. A marketing presence can also make it easier for someone to refer a business. If someone is on the fence about which business to choose, being able to recall some positive messaging can help influence the decision. I know of instances where customers called a business after seeing their commercial vehicle all decaled-up in the parking lot.

4. Online reviews, whether positive or negative, can impact a business. Poor reviews can be fake or planted by competitors, and some can be from real customers but with a skewed experience. For example, store hours might have changed since a customer was last in the business, which causes the customer to feel rushed when making a purchase after being informed of the new hours. It really isn't reflective of the business, but it is something that impacted the 'digital' word of mouth.

A Final Word

Sometimes, when a business doesn't want to deal with marketing, they rely on the '*best advertising is word of mouth*' adage to defer making a decision. If you catch yourself saying or thinking that, it is because something is keeping you from making a decision. Addressing the real issue—cost, not sure what to say, being unfamiliar with online promotion, etc.—will help you make a better decision than not making one at all.

4

I Don't Have Time for Marketing

One of the overwhelmingly common responses I get from business owners when the topic of marketing comes up is, '*I don't have time for it.*' Business owners are among the busiest sector of people I know, and understandably so. You manage a lot of things, and your day rarely goes as planned. A delayed shipment, an absent employee and a computer update can all change the course of your scheduled day. However, even during the chaos, you make time for other things, so why not marketing?

The answer: you make time for important things, and sometimes marketing just doesn't make the cut.

The problem with marketing not being a priority is you end up doing one of two things: 1) you react to promotional opportunities and make a hasty decision, or 2) you delay making any decision at all and do nothing. If you tend towards the former, you can end up with a bad investment for what you spend, because you haven't taken the time to flush out if it's really something worthwhile and effective. If you tend towards the latter and do nothing, it can take longer to return to the forefront of a customer's mind when they're ready to make a purchase. Usually, when a business gets into this situation, they make a reactionary marketing choice, which costs too much and doesn't work. It's a bit of a hamster wheel.

That's the problem with not making time for marketing. To fix the problem, you need to confront the real reason why you aren't choosing to make time for marketing: you don't know what to do. And why should you? You are not a marketing business, you are a home builder, a retail store, an HVAC company, an auto repair shop, etc. You are an expert in your business, not in marketing.

So, what do you do about it?

1. Get Some Help

This is the whole reason why my business exists—I know what to do to help a business with marketing. My clients are people who have tried to do it themselves without success and realize they just can't or don't want to commit the time to doing it, so they contract out the service. I'm less expensive than an employee, and I have an executive-level amount of knowledge to bring to the table. In addition, marketing is a deductible expense! Therefore, at the end of the day, business owners get me for free!

This is exactly how I approach bookkeeping. A professional bookkeeper can do my bookkeeping at a higher level than I can do it on my own. I am not as efficient or as thorough. I don't know it well enough, and I don't want to spend my time learning it to that level. I contract out my bookkeeping, and it gets done on time and correctly, and I get the quarterly reports to review.

If you have access to a marketing consultant, try them out.

2. Make Time

There's no way around it; you must make time for marketing. It's what drives customers through your door, so it matters that you carve out some time to do it. If you commit to doing it yourself, get a calendar and make a plan. (Refer to the marketing plan template in this book for help.) It is important that you follow through to get the most value from the time you will spend, so be sure you do that.

I once heard an explanation about the '*I don't have time*' excuse that we all give to something in our lives. It might be about joining a gym, taking a course, or walking after dinner every evening. Instead of saying, '*I don't have time,*' you should say, '*I don't choose to spend my time doing that.*'

I tried saying that myself a few times, and it really puts things into perspective. It moves you from knowing you *should* do something, to actually *doing* it. I'm a busy person, but I always choose how I spend my time, and sometimes I could make better choices to get where I want to be. It's up to me what I choose.

Like pretty much everything when it comes to owning a business, the buck always stops with the owner. Marketing is the same; whether you do it or not, the responsibility is still yours.

5

Advertising with Your Competition

Advertising is a way to promote your business to a mass group of people. Whether it's a billboard, a radio commercial, or a Facebook ad, many advertising options are available to you. They are the same options also available to your competitors. Should you be advertising in the same space where your competitor is also advertising?

There are cases when it makes sense and cases when it doesn't.

When It Makes Marketing Sense

The case where it makes sense is if the advertising opportunity is targeted to your audience. A good example of this is a travel industry publication.

In travel guides, you see similar businesses advertising in the same publication. The pages contain multiple accommodations providers, restaurants, and attractions. Businesses in this industry understand that the first objective of tourism is to attract people to the region. To do that, there must be substantial regional activities and accommodations. Tourists may not visit your region because of your restaurant, but they may come to your restaurant because they are looking at things to do in the area while they are there. For tourism, advertising with the competition is a good decision, because you are working together to attract people to your region.

When It Makes Financial Sense

Advertising in the same space as your competition can also be a smart financial decision.

One of the publications my agency managed was a health magazine, which was created as a way to market health businesses in the local county which is comprised of 17 small-population towns.

As a rural area, every town does not have every healthcare service that someone might need, so it is common for people to travel to other towns to access a chiropractor, for example. If they have a long drive to and from work, they might be searching for a chiropractor in the town where they work as opposed to the town where they live.

Most of the 17 towns have their own media outlets and advertising mechanisms - so advertising in every community wasn't financially viable for many healthcare services. No one-size-fits-all solution existed, until we made one.

The health magazine was one publication we distributed across the entire 17-community region. Instead of figuring out how to advertise in different communities, there was one place to advertise that was distributed to all the communities. In addition, the magazine's focus was strictly on health, so the audience was exactly the kind of person healthcare clients needed to reach. Businesses were able to cover more ground for less cost in a publication geared to their industry.

When It Doesn't Make Sense

There are also cases when it is not advisable to advertise with your competition. This will be the case if you can't stand out enough in the same space.

Another project for our agency was an online job board called Ottawa Valley Jobs. To expand our marketing, we considered creating a radio ad that would drive people to the website and build awareness of the advertising opportunity for local employers.

On the very morning I had planned to call the radio station to inquire about rates, my administrative assistant heard a commercial on that station for Ottawa Valley Job Shop—another online job board! I did a little research and found the 'job shop' website was like a classified ad option for radio stations - hundreds of 'job shops' existed as a way for radio stations to earn income with website sales.

In this case, I decided not to advertise on the radio station for two reasons. First, my product and their product had nearly identical names, and it was just too close for people to differentiate which one was which. It was likely that my advertising would only elevate my competitor's job board. Second, with the media outlet owning the competing product, they had an unlimited budget for promotion, and it would be too difficult to compete effectively by advertising there. I decided to stay away from all radio and put our efforts into other forms of promotion.

I found new ways to promote that helped elevate our brand. As our product was well-established in the community, the radio ads for the competing product actually increased traffic to our website! Eventually, the radio station abandoned that project, and we continued with other methods of promoting the website.

Two Questions to Ask

Take some time to think about the advertising opportunity when your competitors are involved and ask yourself these two questions:

1. Does the advertising opportunity reach a target audience (group of people) who would be good for your business?

2. If you participate in this advertising opportunity, can you differentiate yourself from others who may be offering the same or similar-type services?

If you answered yes to both questions, it might be worth a try. If you answered no to either question, better opportunities could be out there for you.

27

6

Giving Is Marketing Too

If you have been in business for any amount of time, you have likely been asked to donate to a community event or sponsor an initiative. In some cases, you may wish to simply donate without receiving any acknowledgement of your contribution, and there is nothing wrong with that. While this is a charitable aspect of your business, it is also a marketing opportunity, and there are ways you can make the most of it.

Sponsorships

When you sponsor an event, the event organizer will likely have a list of ways you will be promoted. One option they may have is to promote you on the organization's social media channels, so if you are on Facebook, for example, be sure to follow the organization's page and share the post that tags you as a sponsor. Another way you can market through social media beyond your post is to share when other sponsors are mentioned. You might make a post that reads, *Happy to join ABC Company in supporting this great community cause.* Following the event, you can also make a social media post to congratulate the organization on their success and note that you were again happy to be connected to it.

If the event offers signage, ask for an option to provide some of your own signage as well. The organizers assemble a package based on what they think will work best, but don't be afraid to make some additional suggestions. You may have an idea they had not thought to include, and it could be a win-win for you and the organization. In a golf tournament I was involved with, a car dealership sponsored a hole, and we created a sign for them. They also asked to bring a vehicle to the hole and had their own sign by the vehicle. It was a request we could accommodate, and it added something to the event at the same time.

Sometimes events can offer a group of tickets to a sponsor. If you cannot attend the event or cannot use all the tickets, consider running a ticket giveaway. The event might also help promote your giveaway, and local media may be interested in it as a marketing opportunity for them. You can also seek out suppliers and businesses you work with, or use the tickets as an employee reward, further benefiting from the promotional value of this aspect of your sponsorship. Another idea is to provide the tickets to another non-profit organization and allow them to run a promotion for the tickets you are providing.

Use your sponsorship opportunities as much as possible. Events love when sponsors push their message because it helps market the event. When you are an active sponsor, two things happen: 1) you can often negotiate some additional benefits if you sponsor the event annually, and 2) other events will seek you out to support their initiatives, which can provide you with more choices on what events best serve your marketing and charitable purposes.

Donated Prizes

When donating a prize to an event, take some time to make a great presentation. Often the donated prizes will be on display or used for a raffle, so people will be browsing what is available for them to win. You can make a great impression on everyone, not just the prize winner, when you present something attractive. Here are some ways you can do that:

The Gift Basket

If you are using corporate swag (i.e.: coffee mugs, hats, pens, etc.), put it in a gift basket with some additional items. Add some coffee to go with the mugs or sunscreen to go with the hat. Package it in a nice gift basket wrapped with cellophane. The cellophane not only enhances the look of the basket but also protects the prize. Ensure your business card is prominently displayed, either attached to the outside or included in a high-viewing spot inside the cellophane.

The Gift Card

One of the easiest ways to donate is with a gift certificate or a gift card. Often, they are in a white, unmarked envelope and lay flat on the table. Your gift card donation should be accompanied by your business card and a brochure of your services. Include it in the envelope and put the envelope in a gift bag with some tissue paper and make a statement with it.

For businesses that cannot donate their own services (i.e.: insurance company or realtor), contribute a gift card from a local business. Always include your own information, as you are the one donating the prize. You can even include a small card that states, *"we're happy to contribute to this fundraiser by donating a gift card to ABC Restaurant and encouraging people to shop locally."*

For both options, you have also created an additional marketing opportunity. Take a photo of your gift basket or gift card presentation and share it on your social media pages. Tag the event or the business where you purchased the gift card. When you shop locally for these items, you are more likely to get the local business to also participate in your social media post.

The Coupon

If you are providing a coupon to the participants at an event, take the time to make a good presentation with it. A coupon can be a great, low-cost contribution to an event, and if done properly, it can bring in some business to you as well.

31

There are two keys to an effective coupon: 1) a good offer, and 2) a good presentation.

As a general rule, a percentage-off coupon should at least cover the taxes. If you want to draw more business, increase the percentage to 20 or 25 percent. You can use the coupon to drive business, so consider what you want to accomplish with the offer. If you are choosing a dollar amount discount (i.e.: $10 off), the same idea applies. The more generous you are, the more you will drive business.

The other factor that helps drive business is how your coupon looks to a recipient. Please resist the urge to print your own coupons on copy paper and cut them to size yourself. While that might be the cheap and easy option, trust me, it looks cheap when you do it that way. The coupon is an invite to your business; if it looks like you didn't put much thought into it, you won't get much in terms of a result.

Here is how to create a cost-effective coupon idea that provides big impact at a low cost:

Ideas for a Cost-Effective Coupon

1. Have a professional coupon generic template created for a regular letter-sized sheet of paper. Choose something you can use for multiple giveaways such as *'save $10'* or *'save 20 percent'*. You can have three to four rectangular coupons, or you can create business card-sized coupons, whatever you like. Leave the expiry date space blank so you can fill that in for each event.

2. Print the coupon on cardstock (heavier paper, like a business card). This helps ensure that no one can easily duplicate your coupon, and it feels substantial when someone picks it up.

3. Use a paper cutter to cut your coupons so they will have clean, straight edges. When you use a professional printing service, they will do this for you, but you can purchase a cutter and do it yourself if you want.

The organization you contribute to will take whatever you give them, so putting in the extra effort when it comes to donations is something that helps your marketing. If you are committing to a charitable initiative, why not get some marketing miles out of it too?

As an added benefit, if you are a small business with employees, it can be a great morale boost for employees to know you've created the kind of workplace that contributes to the community. They might even bring some ideas forward for consideration, which can present more opportunities to get your business in front of people who could become your customers. The community will also recognise you as a business that gives back. While this may draw more requests to your door, you can always decide on the initiatives you will support. If more people are knocking, more people recognise you as someone who is a community contributor, and that's good for business.

Download A Quick Reference to Sponsorship and Donations for free!

www.forwardthinkingbook.com

7

The Reluctance to Change

Marketing frequently involves making a change. After all, the goal of marketing is to make people aware of what you do, so if the current methods of doing that are not working, you must change something if you want to make a different impact. As Albert Einstein said, *"Insanity is doing the same thing over and over again and expecting different results."*

While you, the business owner, might be on board with making changes, understand that others in the business may not share your enthusiasm. For example, employees develop a routine when it comes to doing their job, and something that alters that routine makes them feel uncomfortable, so they resist the change. Partners in the business can also be resistant to changes because that change may impact a personal relationship. Taking the time to address the anxieties surrounding change can go a long way towards achieving better results in your marketing efforts and in understanding those relationships important to your business.

Here are some reasons why people can be resistant to change:

Unfamiliar Territory

At the top of the list of reasons why people resist change in marketing is they don't understand why the change is necessary. Marketing is not as straightforward as math, where two apples plus two apples equals four apples. Marketing involves understanding how people behave, where they find information, and what influences them to make decisions. This information is often at odds with what people in the business think customers *should* do, and because it seems unusual, there is resistance to accept it.

Solution

Marketing is about attracting others. To do that, you must reach people by addressing the issue for them. Let your employees know that while we may have to do something different to get customers to learn about what the business can offer, once we get them interested, we can explain the other benefits. For example, you know your plumbing business provides a better quality of service than your competitors. However, the customer may be focused on getting their plumbing work done quickly, so the marketing message might highlight fast, efficient service. Once the customer inquires, you can educate them on the quality of service you provide and other important benefits to close the sale. Marketing brings someone to your door, and to do that, it needs to address an issue that matters most to them, even if it is not the most important issue in the mind of the business.

Past Experience

Most businesses have tried other kinds of marketing initiatives in the past. If they didn't work, there can be resistance to invest in marketing again.

Solution

The question you ask in this situation is "why?" Why didn't the marketing give you the results you wanted last time? I worked with an organization that wanted to increase their fundraising initiatives, so they launched a new event. They ran it one year and never ran it again. It raised $9,500, and they were hoping to raise $50,000. When I delved into their past experience, I found they had set their expectations based on what another organization in the community had raised. What they didn't consider was that when the other organization started their fundraiser, they also raised a smaller amount. They only raised $50,000 after ten years of persistence. In this case, the starting expectation was the reason why the organization was not successful.

The Comfort Zone

People working in your business have a certain way of doing things, especially if they have been in that role for a while. When something is introduced that could change that process, they may become uncomfortable with that change and show some resistance to implementing this new idea. It is common for a level of discomfort to occur in trying something different; the key is to ensure the resistance isn't negating your efforts to build your business.

<u>Solution</u>

As part of a marketing strategy for an employment services client, our marketing research found that while employers knew about the agency, they didn't really know all the services they provided. To help build that awareness, I suggested the administrative assistant could send a personal email to businesses that were advertising for employees to let them know about some of the services in case it was helpful. The employee felt that was too invasive; she didn't want to bother businesses that had not contacted the agency first. Even when presented with the text of the email, she resisted. Although tasked to do the work, she did not send the emails. The manager was reluctant to mandate that the (strong-willed) employee send this email. I suggested that the manager send the email, and if a business expressed interest, the employee could do the follow-up. The manager and the employee agreed.

Almost immediately, the manager received requests for information from the businesses targeted by email. They were very interested in the programs and wanted more information. I had the manager forward the email to the administrative assistant so she could see the language that was used and how the business reacted to it. The administrative assistant very diligently followed up on sending the information and was happy to be helping so many businesses. After a couple of months, the administrative assistant agreed to take on the role of emailing the businesses to make the communications more efficient, and having seen the success of the marketing, she was now eager to do it. As businesses replied positively, she felt proud to generate these new customers for the agency.

Marketing is About People: Internally and Externally

Most businesses consider marketing as an exercise to reach people outside the business (i.e.: potential customers). In addition, marketing also has an impact within the business. While you, as the business owner, are the decision maker, communicating clearly with employees and partners can significantly help your marketing efforts. Your people are ambassadors for your business; you want them to be supportive of what you are doing. If they're not, it can impede your progress.

One of the most impactful statements I ever heard about change was in a workshop I attended about how our thinking can be limited by the things we believe about certain situations. When discussing why people eventually accept change, the facilitator said, "*People change when the fear of change is less than the fear of staying the same.*"

A business owner can choose to stay the same for a long time, even if it results in a drop in revenue. But when the revenue drops too much and more competitors come on the scene, the fear of staying the same becomes a bigger threat to the business's viability than the fear of making a change.

As the owner, you bear 100 percent of the responsibility for the viability of your business. That sometimes means making tough decisions that others in the business may not fully understand. Recognise that they have fears too, and while it is ultimately your decision, first do what you can to calm those fears, then when you're ready to make the change, be committed to doing it.

8

Addressing Negative Comments

Most of the time, marketing is about planning so you aren't faced with pressure to react to an opportunity. However, sometimes you must react, especially if you are facing a negative situation. It could be a negative comment on your Facebook page, a poor review, or a disparaging remark in traditional media. If you face one of these situations, knowing how to handle the situation can alleviate the stress of a negative experience.

Step 1: Decide if You Need to Address the Negativity

You first must decide whether the negative situation is worth your effort to respond. If it is a casual criticism, it might not be worth your time, or someone else might take care of it for you with a positive comment. Every negative comment is not worth addressing; sometimes the commenter is only hoping to get your goat for their own enjoyment.

Others may not realize that the manner in which they made their comment had such a negative tone. If it's not a big deal, consider letting it go.

An Example

I was working with an organization that held an annual dinner event fundraiser. They decided to move venues one year, because the regular venue had double booked for the weekend, and the organization wanted to keep the same weekend as usual. The event was successful with the changed venue.

The organization shared photos of the event on social media, thanking everyone for attending. One person commented that the decor was really terrible, and they couldn't believe how poorly embellished the event had been; they expected more from the organization. Several people replied, suggesting the individual could join the decor committee, coming to the organization's defence that they did an excellent job and the like. The negative commenter apologized for the comment and said she meant no disrespect.

Step 2: If You Do Respond, Make a Statement

If you decide that you need to address the negative comment, make a statement. It should be concise, state the facts, and invite people who have concerns to contact someone in the business. If you're concerned about an overflow of emails, don't be; only people with legitimate concerns will contact you, and you want to communicate with those people. Being open to speaking more about the situation is helpful.

Step 3: Publish Your Statement

You can publish your statement on your own website and social media pages, and you can use it to comment on other pages where individuals are speaking negatively about you. When you post it, you have control of the message. If the original comment was initiated through the media (i.e.: radio or newspaper), you can send them your statement, but be aware they may not publish or read it, or if they do, they may edit it, which may cause you more challenges. When sending to the media, ask if you can have the statement printed as submitted, and if not, consider not doing it.

An Example

A convoy of trucks visited a business that offered fuel, food, and related services. The convoy was somewhat controversial in nature, and when the media learned about their stop, they said the business was 'hosting' the convoy. This story resulted in hundreds of negative comments, threats to boycott the business and other reactions.

After a few days, the business responded with a statement. They said it was important for them to treat all customers the same, and they treated the convoy members the same as any other customer. While the convoy did ask if they could gather for a media opportunity, the business owner said it was not permitted under local bylaws. The convoy complied and moved on.

43

The business shared the comment on their website and social media channels and did invite the traditional media to print/read the statement; one did, others did not. People stopped talking about it and moved on to something else.

The business addressed the issue in a concise manner and repeated the same message across all channels. While they likely still experienced some negative pushback from people who did not see or were not interested in their message, they have a statement to provide people distribute who make the inquiries.

Step 4: Remain Consistent

A written statement will help you be consistent in your message, not only when you deliver it as noted in Step 3, but also for your staff who may have inquiries from customers in the future. When you repeatedly say the same thing in a short, concise manner, you make your message easier to remember. It also keeps you from getting off track if someone tries to '*egg you on*' and encourage more discussion.

Most people who make negative comments go on incessantly when they do it. Having a minimal statement in response to their lengthy diatribe will also diminish the long-winded negative comments.

There have always been negative people who hide behind computer screens or who whisper at watercoolers, concocting gossipy tidbits about whomever they want. As a business, you cannot control what others say, and engagement with people like this won't help you in any way.

Focus on communicating your own message, consistently and truthfully, and you will prevail in the end as the negative people move on to hate on someone or something else.

A Final Tip

It is not easy to handle negative comments about you or your business. It's personal, and it can really prompt some difficult feelings. Communicating without personal feelings is important in matters like this. People will try to draw emotions from you, because they want that explosive response to justify themselves in their negative comments. It's hard, but it is worthwhile to hold the line on a concise, clear, consistent, and non-emotional statement.

A business that sells and services personal watercraft faced a comment on a public social media group about their service. The commenter slammed the staff and was trying to encourage other people to share their negative experiences. The business owner's son responded to the comment and explained the supply chain challenges during the pandemic were greater than normal and that the commenter could call anytime for a discussion. The commenter bantered back and forth, unwilling to accept anything the owner's son had to say. Still, the owner's son remained calm in his approach.

The owner's son did not reveal he was the owner's son; he just said he worked in the business and that they tried really hard to do right by their customers. The commenter did not know he was the owner's son or that he worked at the business, despite seeming to have talked to everyone there with no success. Finally, another person following the conversation explained that the person speaking for the business was, in fact, the owner's son, and that having known the family for generations, they were professional and pleasant to deal with and offered an exceptional service in the community. The negative commenter immediately stopped commenting.

I commended the owner's son on how well he handled that conversation. He thanked me, but also mentioned how hard it was when someone says negative things like that about your business.

It is hard and it hurts to the core, but that's because you have skin in the game. It's your business, your reputation, and that means something to you. The person on the other side has nothing invested in the situation. They couldn't care less what you feel or what impact their comments have on your business, your employees, or your standing in the community. Choosing to engage with someone like that is like playing a high stakes poker game and letting everyone else bet with your money.

Take the high road. Always.

9

The Two Sides of Risk

If you have been in business for any amount of time, you will know a bit of risk exists in most situations. Whether it's changing to a new supplier, carrying a new product, or expanding a new service, even the best-made plans and projections come with a bit of uncertainty attached to them. Marketing is one of those aspects of business where results are not often easy to evaluate, and it can cause a business to defer deciding on moving forward with an opportunity. Unlike bringing in a new product, where you have tangible results on whether people are buying it, marketing is something that needs to build over time, and the risk is whether to do it or wait until something better comes along. However, there is a risk to deferring as well.

The Risk of Moving Forward

If you are considering expanding your marketing efforts, you have likely arrived at that point by feeling like more people could be your customer if they only knew about you. This can come about from people saying, '*I didn't know you did this*,' or by hearing stories from people of how a competitor didn't fulfill the terms of an arrangement. In my experience, if you have this feeling, there is probably some validity to it. So how do you evaluate opportunities to market your business without a guarantee of the results it will produce?

While we always consider the risk in doing something different, we don't often think of the risk involved with staying the same. Something is always at stake. While you might be comfortable in the marketing you are doing, don't confuse something new with being riskier just because it is different. It is natural to feel uncomfortable about something new.

The Risk of Staying the Same

As marketing takes some time to build, a key consideration must always be what happens if you decide to maintain the status quo. Where will you be six months from now if you decide not to move forward on any marketing initiatives? If you are 'coasting' now in your business, it is not likely that the pace will increase without some effort. Also, while you may be comfortable coasting today, it is likely your pace will decrease, which can cause you to make reactionary decisions that deal with the immediate situation, as opposed to well thought-out decisions that can build sustainability.

Case Study

I had a client who wanted to expand their business in a certain region. They had tried posting online that they were looking for clients in that region, but their posts didn't yield any response. They told some of their current customers they were looking for more customers, but that didn't work either. They were quite sure an opportunity existed in this expansion but were completely unsure of how to reach people there.

The efforts they had pursued on their own were zero-cost efforts. As it was a new market for them, they didn't want to expend any additional funds in case it was not successful. That told me they were not quite convinced the expansion to this area would work, so the first job we had together was deciding whether it was worth their time.

We needed to figure out what success would look like. How many items would they need to sell in order to say, '*This was a success?*' Once we had that number, we reviewed their average sales to current clients. This gave us a ballpark figure of how many clients they would have to attract. Now that we had that number, I suggested we do a pilot project to give the attempt enough time to work. I explained they might have lower sales in the beginning, but following the trend in their business of sales building over time, four months would give it time to show a result. They agreed.

When it came to getting the word out, I recommended we advertise in the community newspaper. The client was quite hesitant, feeling that newspapers were not as valuable as online advertising. I had done some research on the newspaper and explained how, in this community, it was still a valued resource. I had some quotes on advertising costs and showed how it could be a step to building a contact list once they had customers from the area. With some reluctance, they agreed.

I understood that the owners felt this endeavour came with some risk, so by putting a time limit on the risk—four months—it became a more manageable risk for them to consider. Now they knew the risk had an end date if things did not go as well as we had hoped.

We placed the advertising, and it worked better than we had anticipated! They sold well over what they had planned, and sales grew every month with the regular advertising. The owners were very surprised to see those results but certainly welcomed them. It had been worth the risk.

And then something else happened.

As the business expanded to this new community, an opportunity emerged in a neighbouring community that became interested in my client's business as well. That opportunity was developed without any advertising costs and allowed for sales during the same schedule as the initial marketing. By being flexible in the marketing plan, we accommodated additional sales with an additional community in the same schedule.

Evaluating Risk

Without taking that risk, the business would have missed out on a long-term increase in sales. When you're facing a marketing decision that carries some risk, ask yourself:

1. What am I risking to do it?
2. What am I risking if I don't do it?
3. If I go ahead, is there a way I can contain the risk to make it more acceptable?
4. If I don't go ahead, what is the outcome that will prompt me to revisit the risk?

10

Getting Comfortable with Sales

When you become a business owner, you assume the role of head salesperson for your business. This is often not a position that comes naturally; you are an expert in the business, not necessarily in the profession of sales. Talking to people and selling them on your products or services is something you need to do to grow your business, so here is how to become more comfortable in that role.

Reframe the Role

While I was visiting a coworking office, I met an individual who provided video production services. We were both waiting for the manager of the office to take us on a tour, so we struck up a conversation. He indicated that while he currently worked part-time for a company, he wanted to build his own business and work with entrepreneurs. He confessed that he wasn't very good at selling himself. I asked him some questions about the kind of work he did, and before too long, we were well-engaged in a conversation. He was a reserved person, but in a short time, it was obvious that he knew what he was talking about in how video production could benefit an organization.

When our conversation ended, I suggested he could reframe the sales role to be more of an information sharing role—tell people what you do in case they might need that service or know someone who might need that service. Sharing information feels less daunting than selling.

Ask Questions

One of the things I noticed about business owners who are nervous about selling themselves is they rarely take the opportunity to learn about the person they are speaking with. Asking a few questions of the other person might provide a great segue to discuss your business. In the example above, when the gentleman said he provided video production services, I asked if he worked for a specific industry. That gave him the opportunity to expand on what he did, which led him to say he wanted to work with entrepreneurs. That provided me with a segue to introduce my business; I also work with entrepreneurs, including small businesses in small towns. That led us to talking about how the rural communities were growing and how you didn't have to be in a major city centre to work.

Asking questions shows you have an interest; it provides opportunities to connect with someone once you know more about them, and it takes some of the pressure off when discussing your business.

Be Who You Are

Many great salespeople are gregarious and outgoing and have no problem at all talking about themselves or their business or suggesting why you should be their newest customer. That's a wonderful skill to have, but it isn't the only way to sell yourself.

I worked with a client who wanted to hire someone to do the sales work for her business. Her true joy was in making the product, and she would have preferred not to be the face of the business. What I learned in working with her was that most of her career prior to becoming an entrepreneur had been in a role where people came to her; someone would call or walk into the office, and she would help them. She never had to seek out a customer. So initially, I did the reaching out to set up some meetings, that we attended together. Once at the meetings, she answered all the questions, which were all about getting more information on the product and how it could be delivered to the organization. All she did was what she had always done: provide information, solve problems, and help. In the end, she was the one selling the products without even realizing it, because all she did was answer questions.

When you're applying for a job, employment coaches talk about transferrable skills—things you have learned in one job that you can reframe and use as a benefit in another role, even if you don't have direct experience in this new role. Business owners have plenty of transferrable skills when it comes to communicating with people. Just because the situation is different doesn't mean your skills aren't still valuable.

Handling a No

When I ask businesses who their customer is, it is not unusual for the reply to be, *"Everyone can be my customer."* Yes, everyone *can* be your customer, but not everyone *will* be your customer. So, when you're introducing your business to someone, accept that while you may think you have a great opportunity to work together, the other person may not feel the same way and could say 'no' to moving forward. While that might feel disappointing, most times when they say no, it has nothing at all to do with you or your product.

I have had people say no to me because of a political agenda. Others turned down a proposal because they wanted to hire their friend's daughter or a family member instead. A board of directors declined an opportunity because they didn't understand how marketing worked and didn't want to appear unknowledgeable, so they just avoided the discussion. Another business was on the edge of bankruptcy and ended up closing its doors a month after we talked. There are many, many reasons why someone says no to your business, and most of the time, it will have nothing at all to do with you.

In presenting fundraising ideas to a local community group, there was significant push back on two of the activities that has the best awareness-building opportunities. Initially, those who were unsupportive of these two activities were vague in their reasoning, saying they just didn't think it would be successful. As others around the table started getting on board with the two ideas, the individuals pushing back finally admitted that they just didn't want to volunteer their time doing either of those activities. In this case, the ideas had merit and would bring good awareness to the organization, but some of the volunteer members did not want to participate in those activities, which caused the organization not to continue with them. That decision didn't diminish the value of the ideas at all–it just didn't fit what the volunteers were willing to commit to do.

While a 'no' can be disappointing, it's not personal. It just means it's not a good fit—not right now and maybe not ever—so accept it and put your time towards growing opportunities as opposed to figuring out closed doors. Sometimes that works itself out with a change in leadership or a change in direction.

A Secret Tip

Often when you are in a meeting with a potential customer, they make a request that you know you cannot deliver but the customer seems intent on having it as part of the deal. If you confront this situation, it can put the deal in jeopardy—or, at least, turn a congenial meeting into a disruptive one. If you find yourself in this situation, do two things:

1. Ask some questions about the request and find out why it matters so much to them.

2. Ask if you can do some thinking on it, as it is something new, then get back to them.

Asking Questions

A client of mine sold frozen meals to seniors' organizations that were dealing with an out-of-town supplier. One organization asked if the client would consider new packaging that matched the out-of-town supplier, because it allowed them to stack meals easily in their freezers.

The client did not want to change her packaging, but also didn't want to say 'no' to the customer, so we asked some questions about how the process worked with the out-of-town supplier. What we discovered was the out-of-town supplier had a minimum order requirement for frozen meals, and the customer had figured out a way to maximize the freezer space with the larger-than-necessary orders. Basically, it was a warehousing issue. As a local business, my client offered a service without a minimum order requirement, so it eliminated the warehousing issue. The customer was happy about the flexibility of the customized order option and signed on with my client.

Getting Back

In a magazine I publish, a business asked if they could include a flyer in the magazine as a special insert. While newspapers and larger magazines have the capacity to do this, as a one-person operation, I didn't. I asked to get back to them on the request. After a few days, I explained I would have to hire someone to open every box of magazines, insert a flyer into every magazine, then re-pack the boxes, and we simply didn't have the manpower to do that. However, I could include the brochure as a two-page spread in the magazine, saving them money and still accomplishing the goal of having their information in the publication. They opted not to advertise.

Six months later, they asked if the two-page spread was still an option and booked it for an upcoming issue.

Being a salesperson is about making life better for people by introducing them to your product or service. Some people will take you up on that, others will not. Nobody sells everybody everything, and that's okay.

11

When Competitors Copy Your Ideas

Nothing's better than coming up with a great promotion. You get everything in place, launch it, and see results from your hard-earned efforts. Then one day, you notice your competitor has copied your idea and is doing the same thing.

It's aggravating for sure, but it isn't as threatening to your business as you might think. Here's why:

They Don't Know What They Don't Know

First, you took the time to plan this promotion. You contemplated a lot of factors and added or edited some of the original plans to make a final decision. Your competitors didn't do that work, so they don't know what's all behind it. Maybe you capitalized on a purchasing deal from a supplier or found a new way to combine services you already offer.

You might be pushing to meet a quarterly target, or the promotion could be part of a larger strategy to grow an aspect of your business. You have also considered the cost and how you will sustain the traction of the promotion. Your competitor doesn't know any of these things, so by simply copying what you're doing, they're leaving a lot of the outcome to chance. That's not a great strategy to grow a business.

While the competitor may pull some interest their way, it won't be enough to threaten the success of your promotion. If the competitor cannot live up to the promise of the promotion—price, longevity, additional benefits—they may even be sending customers your way.

You Establish Yourself as a Leader

You never have to worry about your competitor being in the lead if they are always following you, and that gives you an advantage in the market. While the competitor is focused on what you're doing, you are focused on growing your business.

For example, two plumbing businesses may offer similar services, but one business may have five employees, and another may have ten. One service may have a niche in commercial work, while the other might be entirely residential. One may have a 24/7 emergency option, while the other business may not. Just because businesses offer the same products and services you provide doesn't mean they operate the same way.

When you plan your marketing with a strategy to grow your business, it is focused on *your* business and highlighting the strengths, benefits, and opportunities that you bring to the marketplace. Keeping that focus on your own business will allow you to reap the benefits marketing provides. When you try to follow someone else, you'll never be in a position of leading your business growth.

Is There a Legitimate Impact?

There may be cases where it is worth addressing the problem of a competitor who has copied your idea. As a marketing agency, the creative work I do for clients is protected by copyright.

In one instance, I wrote a radio ad for a client, and soon after, the radio station used the same language for another business. I contacted the radio station to let them know it was original content and that they couldn't just replace my client's name with another business. They apologized and removed the other ad. When the radio station creates ads for clients, they have the copyright of that work and can reuse it with their clients. In this case, they didn't know an outside ad agency had designed the ad making it off-limits for them to reuse.

In another instance, I designed a print ad for a client promoting a product they had recently added to their business. The client called me a month later and said a competitor had duplicated the ad in the newspaper. The newspaper had just removed my client's logo and contact details and replaced them with the competitor's information. I informed newspaper that this was copyrighted artwork. They removed the competitor's ad.

When evaluating whether to pursue a solution to having a competitor copy your marketing, you must decide whether the copy is threatening your business or if it's just irritating. Most of the time, it will just be irritating.

As a creative agency, many of my ideas are copied by other media and advertising outlets. For those that infringe on copyright, I address them. However, for those copied ideas where the outlet is trying to make a quick buck, I shrug them off. None of those copied ideas has ever been sustainable, because I had a long-term strategy behind the idea and the infrastructure to support it. The other outlets didn't have that foundation, and everything crumbled pretty quickly.

The Strategy Will Pay Off

The moral of this story is to stick with your own strategy. You may make mistakes, but you will learn from them and improve as you move forward. Mistakes make us all better business operators.

Your marketing strategy is a foundation for growing your business, and even if someone stole your entire strategy, they couldn't implement it the same way, because their business operation is not the same. Trust your experience and your strategy and focus on building your business in a sustainable way. Most businesses will not spend the time to do this, so you're already miles ahead of your competitors if you do.

12

Acknowledging Personal Bias

A naïs Nin, an often-cited author, is famously attributed to saying, *"We don't see things as they are, we see them as we are."*

Whenever you do something new or different, you can expect to encounter critics. They may not be loud and in-your-face critics; they could be employees, colleagues, or friends who are doubtful of your ability to successfully do this new thing. When you face this situation, it is important to remember why you wanted to do something new and different in the first place: you want a change. As a business owner, you have an investment in your business that others do not have, so they do not see the situation as it is; they see the situation as it impacts them.

I worked with an organization that answered to a board of directors. My role was to devise ways for the organization to build awareness in the community. The objective was that if more people knew how impactful the organization was, they would support initiatives (i.e.: events, fundraising, etc.) when asked to do so.

We built on several initiatives over the course of a few years, all of which contributed to the goal of making the organization better known in the region. Some of the initiatives raised funds as well, and one was quite unique in that it helped the organization reach a new audience that it had not connected with previously. We ran this initiative for two years with more success than we had anticipated and with growth in the second year. When it came time to plan for the third year, I was surprised to hear two members of the board suggest we should cancel it.

The two board members had not participated in the initiative in the past two years. It was not something they weren't interested in, so they didn't feel it held any value. Even when the case was made for how it helped the agency build awareness, these two board members maintained their position of non-support. The committee voted to discontinue the event.

This was a case of people in a position of decision-making authority who chose to focus on their personal feelings about the initiative as opposed to how it contributed to the goals of the organization. There was also a greater consequence to losing this initiative: another organization picked it up and used it to spread their message and increase support for what they were doing. By making a decision based on a personal feeling, the organization now had to work harder to get their message out.

I tell my clients that my job is to present ideas on how to succeed in what they want to achieve, and their job is to decide what ideas they want to implement. Together, we work to make it happen. Some clients choose to decide when I present it to them, while others like to bring it to their staff, management team or board of directors for comment. There are always personal viewpoints in the external group that conflict with the overall objectives. A staff member might see the idea as something that will make their role busier, so they find a problem with it. A manager might feel like he's losing control of his department, so he finds a challenge to this new idea's implementation. A member of the board may not personally participate in the idea, so they speak against its likely effectiveness.

When facing this kind of discussion, here are some ways to accept the feedback while maintaining focus on the main objectives that the new ideas were brought forward to reach:

1. Acknowledge everyone who participates in the discussion. The worst thing is not that people disagree with your idea; it shows they care about what happens. The worst thing is when people are indifferent to it and don't care one way or the other about what the business decides to do.

2. Ask the person raising the concern if they have a suggestion of how the idea could still move forward while allowing their concern to be met. For the employee concerned about being too busy, ask if

65

they would be willing to let their supervisor know when things were too busy so someone else could help. Empower the critic to be part of their own solution.

3. Offer updates in shorter timeframes. Marketing plans take time to implement, so results don't always show right away. However, you can easily provide an update to the group on what is being done and accomplishments to date. Be sure to recognise the group for their participation in the successful outcomes. You always want people to feel free to share their concerns without experiencing a negative consequence in doing so.

The most important part of embarking on new ideas is to follow through with them. When you can complete an initiative, you let your staff or board members know you are someone who will see things through to the end. Even if the outcome doesn't produce everything you want, you still gained experience, insight, and knowledge that will always help in future initiatives.

Act as if you know you will succeed, and you will often find more successful outcomes than you anticipated.

13

The Value of Knowing Your Best Customers

If you have been in business for any amount of time, this chapter might seem redundant; of course, you know who your best customers are or else you wouldn't still be in business. If you operate a retail store, you might think of your regular customers. If you run a construction company, you might think of your highest-paying customers. When you think of customers off the top of your head, certain ones will come to mind. But what I am encouraging you to do in this chapter is to get a bit more specific about who your best customers actually are, then use that information to have more impactful marketing.

Use Your Customer Information Effectively

I worked with a healthcare client who wanted to target a certain geographical section of town to market her business to the people who lived there. When I asked her why she came to that conclusion, she said she had a few customers from this part of town and thought it would be a good idea to reach out to that area. As my client had a business that recorded a customer's address, I asked her to first do a review of where her customers were coming from, then note the customers who used her services regularly (her best customers). She did that breakdown, and the results showed a very different picture: her best customers were coming from areas that did not have a healthcare clinic in their region. If she wanted to grow her business more efficiently, she needed to target the residents of the communities without her type of healthcare service.

The more information you can gather about your best customers, the better you can gear your marketing initiatives to that kind of person. You can still be open to any kind of customer; there are just certain types of people or organizations who are more likely to be attracted to your business than others. Knowing this information can save you a lot of time and money in marketing.

Finding Niche Opportunities

Another client I worked with had been thinking about how to grow his business for some time and had tried a few things that hadn't yielded much success. When we drilled down on who the best customers were in his business, they were predominantly seniors. With that information, we looked at organizations that connected to seniors and reached out for a meeting to introduce my client's product and how it might work for those organizations.

This was a very specific group, and initially, he had some hesitation, because it seemed like too small of an audience when other venues saw considerably more people. However, what we learned in our meeting was that while there were only five seniors' organizations in the area, they purchased a significant amount of product! If my client could become a vendor with these organizations, the potential for the business was financially significant. Plus, there was far less work on the client's part in terms of marketing the product to the audience.

The result was a win for the seniors' organizations and for the client. It also allowed for a direct marketing approach that was more cost-effective and helped grow other areas of the business as well. A niche audience with the right outreach strategy created a stronger best customer base for the client.

Attracting More of Your Best Customers

Sometimes drilling down on your best customer is less about financial gain and more about the enjoyment of your business. This was the case for my own marketing consulting work.

For many years, I submitted requests for proposal for municipal marketing work. I was very drawn to helping towns communicate better with their residents, businesses, and potential future residents. The proposal forms were time consuming to complete, and I was never selected as the winner of the contract. When I followed up to find out where I had fallen short, there were two main responses: 1) the municipalities preferred to go with a larger firm, and 2) the preference was to deal with people who had worked in the municipal sector as opposed to those with experience in business or other sectors.

At first, this was disappointing to learn, but it was key information that helped me focus on my best customer.

What I enjoyed in my work, and where I was most successful, was working with businesses and organizations that truly wanted to be the best they could be. They were comfortable with thinking outside the box, and they wanted a marketing partner to help grow their business. They valued flexibility, unique ideas, and impact. When we were successful, these clients were happy to refer me to colleagues in other businesses, and that helped grow my business financially.

While I loved the opportunity to make an impact with municipal work, their structure was not as congruent with my strengths. I was more aligned with businesses that often needed a quick turnaround, someone they could trust to run with ideas and get things done. Municipalities have more people in the approval chain than businesses, therefore decisions don't happen as quickly. So, I stopped bidding on municipal marketing proposals. They still tugged at my heart, and I still imagined all the amazing things we could do to make communities better (and maybe one day I'll write a book on that), but my best customers were the decision-makers themselves, and that's where I put my focus.

That's why there is plenty of work for many kinds of businesses in your same field (i.e.: competitors). I have often referred work to other businesses with services that intersect with mine, and they're happy to do it, because that work may be a best customer for them. It might feel strange to turn away a customer, but it's more about putting your time to the person who is *your* best customer. There is a limit on the amount of time we have to service clients, and the more you can spend on your best customers, the happier you will be.

14

Before You DIY Your Design Work

Marketing works to develop the perception that people have of your business, and almost all your marketing involves a visual element. Eighty percent of how we gather information comes through our eyes, so nothing matters more than what your marketing looks like to others. Your signage, business cards, coupons, website, and social media posts are all visual; and people judge by what they see. The urge to save money and do your own graphic work is one of the biggest mistakes business owners make, because not only do you need the tools to do the work, you need the knowledge of how to do it.

Why Visuals Matter

I have had many experiences with businesses and organizations that undervalue visual work. Why does it matter so much? Here are a few things to make you think:

- A study by Ernesto Olivares[1] found that 90 percent of information absorbed by the brain is visual; the other 10 percent is shared by the other four senses. Also, we process visuals 60,000 times faster than text.

- It takes less than two-tenths of a second for an online visitor to form a first opinion about your website, according to researchers at the Missouri University of Science and Technology.[2]

- Our brains crave simplicity and will look for a shortcut for processing information. Visuals allow the brain to process more information in less time.

- The average person gets distracted in eight seconds.[3]

- Visual cues help us to better retrieve and remember information[4]. The brain is mainly an image processor, not a word processor.

- A well-designed visual image[5] can yield a much more powerful and memorable learning experience than a mere verbal or textual description.

- We are hardwired to engage and recognise visual content[6] much more than any other content. There is a high emphasis on how brands create visual experiences for their customers to emotionally connect with them.

---

[1] https://ernestoolivares.com/we-are-90-visuals-beings
[2] https://www.sciencedaily.com/releases/2012/02/120216094726.htm
[3] https://www.spectrio.com/marketing/compelling-reasons-why-visual-marketing-matters-more-than-you-think
[4] https://www.psychologytoday.com/us/blog/get-psyched/201207/learning-through-visuals
[5] https://cft.vanderbilt.edu/guides-sub-pages/visual-thinking
[6] https://www.moxels.com/post/consumer-behaviour-visual-experiences

Being in business, I understand the demands of managing expenses and managing time. Few of us have unlimited money, and none of us has unlimited time. Every decision we make on where to allocate our money or time has a consequence, and making a good impression with a future customer is definitely worth the time and money you spend in the long term. Without customers, there is no business.

A Good List to Reference

Nayomi Chibana, a journalist who researches trends in visual communication, published an article entitled *19 Common Graphic Design Mistakes Made By Non-Designers*[7]. Here is a brief summary of her list:

1. Using too much text instead of visuals.
2. Poor readability: too many words in one line of text.
3. Mismatching fonts that give the design a disorganized and unprofessional look.
4. Bad kerning (space between letters) to allow for more text.
5. Not choosing the right colours.
6. A sure sign of an amateur designer is the lack of white space (negative space) in a visual design.
7. Placing elements arbitrarily can lead to a product that looks messy and disorganized.

---

[7] https://visme.co/blog/graphic-design-rules

8. Not knowing how to use contrast effectively can mean the difference between an effective design and an ineffective one.

9. Not scaling properly and distorting or stretching elements.

10. An important principle of graphic design is visual hierarchy, which communicates to the viewer the importance of each element in relation to the rest.

11. Hard-to-read text.

12. Inappropriate font combinations.

13. Inadequate space between lines (leading). Too much space between lines can cause your text to appear disjointed, while too little space can make the text appear too tight and crowded.

14. Using raster images comprised of pixels, which become blurry when enlarged. Vector images can be scaled to any size and still appear crisp.

15. Striving for complete symmetry.

16. Failing to communicate effectively. You can get so caught up in creating a design that appeals to our own tastes and aesthetic preferences that you forget about the client's needs and, worst of all, about the content and how it should serve its audience.

17. Copying others' work. It is not okay to copy someone else's work and pass it off as your own. You can face a copyright infringement issue if you do this.

18. Forgetting the medium. You need to design differently for online (website) and print. Enlarging a small design or shrinking a large design won't work.

19. Not being consistent. Consistency makes it easier for a reader to remember you.

If there is anything you didn't understand in the above nineteen points, or if you have done some of the things on this list, you should not be doing your own graphic design work.

Avoiding a Legal Situation

I once joined a large committee that had already begun marketing their event. At our first meeting, I saw the event logo and thought it looked familiar. An administrative assistant had designed the logo, and it was already appearing in advertising and promotional materials. I asked where the graphic had come from, and the committee seemed irritated that I was questioning this, given they had already decided upon it and wanted to move forward. Finally, we discovered the assistant had taken the logo from a scanned image of a copyrighted graphic owned by a multinational company. I explained the image was copyrighted (not available for others to use) and that we had to either ask permission from the company to use the image (which was not likely to happen) or we could create our own graphic and be clear of any copyright infringement. It took two meetings before the committee decided to go with artwork we were legally allowed to use.

The administrative assistant didn't know about copyright infringement. She enjoyed making graphics on the computer and offered to create the logo because it was fun to do. The committee lost a few months of work and about $3,000 in promotional materials with the copyrighted image. However, for a half-million-dollar event, they were lucky to only be out that much before rectifying the problem.

The $2,000 Flyer

An organization asked me to quote on designing a flyer for them. I quoted $125 and committed to having it done within twenty-four hours. The organization's receptionist said she could do that flyer for free, so they opted to go with her.

The receptionist took a little longer designing the flyer because she was also doing her receptionist job. Once she finalized it, they bought some special paper and printed it. It came out with a white border around the page when what they wanted was for the colour to go right to the edge of the paper. They tried and tried to make this work but couldn't get the result they wanted.

The following week, the manager contacted me for help. I explained that office printers would always have a white border around a flyer. If they wanted the colour to extend to the whole page (called a bleed), they would need to use a professional printer. I asked if they wanted me to take over the project, but they decided to just send the artwork to the professional printer themselves.

The printer didn't use the DIY program that the receptionist had used, so they had to redesign the flyer. The printer also asked about paper weight and quantity, and even though the receptionist was not familiar with either, she ordered it anyway. She also ordered coloured paper to help the flyer stand out.

The receptionist converted the file to a format that wasn't suitable for printing due to using raster images, and the printer indicated this would not work. However, as the image appeared clear on the receptionist's computer screen, she told the manager that the printer didn't know his job very well and suggested the agency move to another printer. They did.

The receptionist found someone to print what she wanted with the file she had created. When she picked up the order, a white border surrounded the flyer, it wasn't centred and the graphics were blurry.

The coloured paper altered the organization's logo, and the colour of the text wasn't dark enough to show up on bright pink paper, so it wasn't readable. As she had pre-paid for the job, the organization was out the money and still had no flyer.

The manager came back to me and asked me to do the flyer, which I did. Here's how the cost worked out:

<u>Internal Cost</u>

- Receptionist - $540 ($18 per hour x 30 hours)
- Other staff - $240 ($20 per hour x 12 hours)
- Manager's time - $500 ($100 x 5 hours)
- Printing (internal photocopier) - $350
- Printing (other printer) - $275
- **Total internal cost: $1,905**
- **Days to completion: 27 (plus 47 employee hours)**

<u>My Cost</u>:

- Design of flyer: $125
- Printing: $100
- **Total external cost: $225**
- **Days to completion: 1**

I cannot stress enough how important it is that your visual marketing materials look the part. If the person who is doing that work does not make a living from designing professional marketing materials, they are likely the wrong person to work on that job for you. If the person you have chosen is just asking you where you want things to be and not advising you on what is best in attracting the customer, they are also likely the wrong person to work on that job for you.

15

Writing for Your Audience Matters

A *Forbes* magazine article, "Why Writing Ability Is The Most Important Skill In Business (And How To Acquire It)[8]," made the following statement: *Business is fundamentally about getting other people to do things—getting employees to be productive, customers to buy your product or service, government to leave you alone—and you can't make these things happen if you can't communicate well.*

There is a difference between writing and writing with a purpose. If you want to encourage action, you must communicate in a way that impacts the audience to whom you are writing. The challenge is separating the information you know from the information to provide people so they will do something with it. Here is an example:

---

[8]https://www.forbes.com/sites/forbesagencycouncil/2019/01/29/why-writing-ability-is-the-most-important-skill-in-business-and-how-to-acquire-it/?sh=2a0aa1672fdf

Business-Focused Writing

ABC HVAC Services is a locally owned and operated business since 1983. Our goal is to exceed our customers' expectations with trained technicians and superior products. We offer installations, service, and repair of all your HVAC needs, and our employees are certified and insured. We work in a hundred-mile radius of this beautiful region, and our goal is to do work right the first time. When you choose us, you choose quality you can trust.

Audience-Focused Writing

When your air conditioning stops working in the middle of summer, you need someone who can respond quickly. At ABC HVAC Services, we can be on site quickly and get you back to enjoying the comfort of your home. Our trained technicians can isolate the problem and make the necessary repairs, or we can offer a new unit from a trusted brand with a ten-year warranty.

Heating, ventilation, and air conditioning are key factors that make your home enjoyable and efficient. Let us be your first call to fix a problem or upgrade your comfort services.

The customer always wants to know what's in it for them; do you understand their problem, and can you provide them with an efficient and effective solution? If so, they will be prompted to inquire further with you. When you communicate with a certain audience, you must speak your message in a way that resonates with them. Your goal in marketing communications is to attract interest from someone, not to give them an entire history of your business or the purpose and vision of your organization. That information is valuable, but it comes later. Initially, you must be more yielding to the person's needs rather than your own desire to share information you deem as critical to operations. Moreover, it is not an easy task.

Make the time to communicate well. It can be the difference between someone taking the next step in becoming a customer or browsing another service.

16

The Elements of Professional Emails

Much of the way your business communicates today occurs by email. Writing an appropriate business email is critical, as it is a reflection of your business and an important part of your customer service. Here are some tips to share with everyone who is involved in communicating by email for your business.

There is a difference between writing and writing with a purpose. If you want to encourage action, you must communicate in a way that impacts the audience to whom you are writing. The challenge is separating the information you know from the information to provide people so they will do something with it. Here is an example:

1. Addressing the email. When possible, address the person by name. If you don't know the person's name, start with *'Good afternoon'* or another similar option. Avoid the *'To whom it may concern'* line.

2. Boring is better. Use a regular (boring) email font such as Helvetica, Tahoma, Arial, or similar style. Stay away from a script font (cursive). Also, avoid these common email mistakes:

   a. Do not use different colours of text in your email. Keep to black.

   b. If you need to highlight something to draw attention, bold it.

   c. Refrain from using underlines unless you are separating topics in a text.

   d. Emojis, GIFs and other icons should not be included in business writing.

   e. Do not use all caps for any reason.

3. Be polite and concise. Say only what you need to say and include only information of which you are certain. Don't guess about a deadline or delivery or the recipient of the email will hold you to it. As an example: Good afternoon. Thank you for your email about ABC product. We are awaiting our next shipment, and I will contact you when they arrive. If you have any other questions, please let me know. Anne.

4. The subject line. Choose a meaningful subject line that the person can recognise immediately as being connected to an inquiry. Also, good subject lines make it easier for both you and the recipient to find an email for future reference.

5. Use white space. Your paragraphs should be limited in length to make the email easier to read. When too much text is bunched together, the reader may not pick up all the information you are conveying. As a rule of thumb, type three to four sentences in one paragraph. Then make a new paragraph to continue the email.

6. Reference attachments. If you are including an attachment, be sure to reference it in your email. That way, if you forget to attach it, the reader will know right away, and you can resend the email. It is also a reminder to the reader that the information is attached.

7. Call to action. If you want the reader to do something when they get your email, be sure to tell them and be specific. For example, instead of saying, '*Tell me what you think,*' opt instead for, '*Please respond with your preferred meeting time by September 5 at noon.*'

Apologizing by Email

We all make mistakes and have had to issue an apology at some point. Here is a guide on how to issue an apology by email.

• Start by apologizing for the error, mistake, or miscommunication.

• Explain what the appropriate situation is, and add as much detail as is necessary, but don't overstate it.

- Offer a solution or repair to the problem if possible.
- Ask the reader to accept your apology.
- Don't blame anyone else.
- Keep the email to the apology only; don't add information unrelated to the apology.

Here are two examples of an apology (from errors I have personally made with clients):

Example 1:

I am so sorry I missed putting your ad in our latest edition of the magazine. It was a mistake on my part, and I sincerely apologize for it. I would like to offer to run your ad at half price in our next edition to compensate. Please let me know by August 10 if this would work for you. Again, I sincerely apologize for my error.

Example 2:

I am very sorry to have noted your invoice as outstanding, when you are right, it was paid. I apologize for the time it took you to look into that for me, and I want you to know I have immediately noted the payment details. I really appreciate your response.

Every Email is a Marketing Opportunity

Whenever you or one of your employees sends an email, it is creating a perception of how you do business. If you have ever had an experience communicating with an automated system, you know how aggravating it can be when the problem you present isn't in the database of the non-human responding to you.

When you write your own emails, you have an opportunity to convey a personal communication, and people greatly appreciate it as our society becomes more automated. Use email as a free marketing tool to build the profile of your service levels to customers. Everyone appreciates good service.

17

The Secret to Dealing with the Competition

Before I started Forward Thinking, I had a career as a golf professional. I played at some of the highest levels of women's professional golf, where my income was determined by the number of competitors I could beat that day. The only result that counted was my score.

The scoreboards around the course served as reminders of how many people were playing better than I was playing, and every missed putt had a price tag on it. It was an intense career built on how to compete at your best when it counted, and it was my best training ground to become a business owner.

What I learned was that business is an even more competitive arena.

Play Your Own Game

In professional golf, you play for your income, but you can also have sponsors and hold fundraisers to help raise money. When you open a business, no one will sponsor you or hold a fundraiser for you; you must make it on your merits every single day. You have to win over customers when businesses around the block or around the world are also vying for those dollars. So how do you manage the competition in your business? It starts by playing your own game.

You have very little, if any, control over the competition. You cannot prevent someone from opening a competing business or from advertising on the same radio station where you also advertise. You do not control their marketing budget, the events they support, or how they spend their money on any facet of their business. You cannot control if they are richer or bigger than you. As you cannot control any of these factors, don't waste your time monitoring what they are doing. Put your time on what you can control: your own business.

Competitors Can Work to Your Advantage

Build your business (and your marketing) on your strengths. No one business can be everything to everyone, so knowing what you do best is a great niche to carve out for your business. When I started my business, there were no other marketing firms in the region. Within ten years, twenty-five or more people were promoting that they too were marketing specialists. I was aware of them, and I visited their websites to learn their credentials. In every case, I found none of them had my education, experience, or competitive background. I promoted my strengths to attract a client who valued those traits, and it resulted in more long-term contracts. What I lost were customers who wanted a cheaper option: $75 for a new logo or $100 to set up a Facebook page. I was grateful those customers had someone to go to for those jobs, because it allowed me to focus on the longer term and more financially rewarding contracts that helped me grow my business.

Carve Out Your Niche

It's up to you if you want to match a promotion that a competitor is running, but you can build your business just fine if you don't. A client of mine had a competitor who decided to aggressively target his customers. The competitor offered to provide the same service at a lower price. When a customer called my client to see if he would match the price, my client declined and explained he was confident that his price matched the quality of service he provided. When the customer said they were switching providers, my client wished them well and thanked them for their past business.

My client was concerned this would impact his business in the long term, so we looked at the customers who had been switching. We found they were all small-income customers, and while they were important to my client's business, it wasn't a revenue loss that warranted changing his business pricing and service strategy, at least, not at this point. The competitor had approached a few of his higher-level customers, and they opted not to change based on how they valued the relationship with my client, which was a combination of price, service, and availability.

This situation continued for about a year. Meanwhile, my client built his business with more clientele that valued the full relationship: price, service, and availability. Despite losing some customers, his business grew financially. Then some of the customers who had chosen the cheaper service started calling my client, wanting to return. While the competitor's lower price was great, some service issues arose, and it impacted their ability to operate. My client took back some of the customers who had treated him well when they parted ways, but for those who scolded him on his pricing, he said he just didn't have room for them. It was an opportunity to focus on the growth areas of his customer base, which, in turn, grew his business.

Competition Can Help a Good Business

I understand it is never a good feeling to have a competitor challenge your business. It hurts when a customer chooses someone else over you, especially if you have always treated them well and maybe even gone the extra mile for them a time or two. However, competition can be a way for you to get specific about the kind of customer who has the biggest impact on your business, and it can help you focus on how to attract that specific customer type. It also lets you focus on your strengths and do the things that set you apart from the competition.

While the competition will always exist in your tenure as a business owner, your business isn't about them; it's about you. The competition is irrelevant to your success. Play your own game and drive your own results.

"Competition whose motive is merely to compete, to drive some other fellow out, never carries very far. The competitor to be feared is one who never bothers about you at all, but goes on making his own business better all the time."–Henry Ford

18

Give Your Marketing Time to Work

One day, I was scrolling through Facebook, and I saw a post from a restaurant that was looking to expand delivery into a nearby community. This was their post:

Tomorrow is our second attempt at delivery to ABC Community. Honestly, I thought we would have a little more interest, but maybe not many people know I exist. So, this is the last chance. Let's share and make this happen, people. Reminder, this is only a trial run.

The 'tomorrow' wasn't successful either. The problem with this attempt to grow the business was not the product or the nearby community. The problem was in how it was marketed.

Marketing Needs Time

The post noted that they had tried one other time to deliver to the nearby community and likely didn't deliver, because there were no orders. One or two attempts at something like restaurant delivery won't cut it. The restaurateur needed to commit to three or four months of delivery. You must give people time to try you out.

The restaurateur blamed people a little for the unsuccessful first attempt. It is never the customer's fault if they don't support you! If people don't know you exist, you need to get the word out so they do know you exist. A Facebook post is not enough to encourage customers to do business with you.

The comment about it being the last chance for people to benefit from the service was truly the nail in the coffin. Again, it comes across as blaming the customer for the failed attempts, and that will never win you any future business. I cannot stress enough how the responsibility of building a customer base is 100 percent on the shoulders of the business owner. People are not obligated to become your customer because you hang up a shingle and are open for business. You must convince them that you are worth their time and money. Blaming them for not supporting you won't achieve that.

Finally, the post ends with a reminder that the delivery is a trial run. In other words, the restaurateur has no plan to commit to it. So, why would someone in a nearby community get excited about ordering from this restaurant only to have delivery stop? If the business is not committing, why should the customer?

People Need Time to Make a Change

The story of the restaurateur is not uncommon; most businesses do not stay long enough at the new venture to become successful. In smaller communities, it can take a long time for people to catch on and try something new, so you really have to commit to it. The benefit of committing is that once you start to win people over, you will have them for a long time, and that will make it more difficult for a competitor to enter your space.

Here are some things to consider when venturing into a new space, launching a new product, or determining how long to stick with something:

1. Have a solid foundation of information about what you want to do and how many people could be your potential customers. If your foundation is that a few friends think it's a good idea, don't do it. You need to know the customer base is there to support you.

2. Know your financial commitment to keep going. You will have some costs to pursue this new direction, but you will also have some costs to maintain it for a period of time. Decide what you are willing to commit financially. This will help you feel less stressed about getting business and will allow you to be more proactive in making good decisions on getting the word out.

3. Have a plan on how you will promote this new initiative and stick to it. A plan will give you something concrete to do on a regular basis to keep the information circulating. It will also give you a good marketing workout to ensure you are truly committing to putting in the time to make this a success. Also, ensure your plan has a good mix of marketing ideas: social media, personal outreach, networking, etc. Don't put all your ideas in one medium; use a variety of communications to see what will connect best with people.

4. Evaluate fairly. So many people walk away from success right before they reach it. If you didn't do all the things in your marketing plan, be honest about it. If something ended up costing more than you anticipated, be honest about that. You may need to revamp your idea instead of throwing it out. If you have a good foundation of information, it might be worth sticking with it just a little longer.

There is no guarantee that trying something new will yield success, but even if the new thing doesn't work out, you can learn a lot about the experience that can help you in other aspects of your business. Sometimes the people who truly need your help and the people you know could benefit from your help are simply not ready to be your customer. From that experience, you will learn what makes someone ready to be your customer, then you market to those people. Trying new things always presents an opportunity for those willing to take it!

19

The Efficiency of Experts

As a business owner, it can feel like your job description encompasses everything. You are responsible for sales, public outreach, marketing, accounting, human resources, event organization, and the list goes on. While you are responsible for these things, you do not have to be the expert in all these things; you can find others to help you.

The first expert I hired in my business was a bookkeeper. She looks after my quarterly government remittances and end-of-year financials, while I do the invoicing and collecting payments. When I had employees, I also had her do the payroll information. I know I could have learned how to do that work, but I wouldn't be as efficient at it as someone who is an expert in bookkeeping. In addition, I would rather spend my time with billable client work than non-billable paperwork.

My bookkeeper also provides me with a quarterly summary of my business's financial situation. I have used this to determine how I can be more efficient in the financial aspect of my business. For example, I used to claim a lot of restaurant meals, but they were only a 50 percent deduction. So, I moved to more breakfast and coffee meetings as opposed to lunch and dinner with that information. My expenses review also helped me decide when to make purchases, such as a new laptop and printer. Having that information is strategic in maximizing the financial decisions of my business. Plus, bookkeeping is a business deduction.

My marketing consulting work is also a business deduction. While all deductions are still an upfront expense, it can be a financially strategic option to use contracted services to help achieve better results in your business.

For example, I had a client who had always handled her own marketing work. As her business expanded, she consulted with me on how to promote in a certain region. We decided the best way forward was to run some advertising with a local media outlet. I asked if she wanted me to look after it, but she decided to do it herself from that point.

She emailed the media outlet for some advertising information. A few days later, I received an email from her with some questions that the advertising rep had asked. It was about the size of the ad and the content. I advised her on both and asked if she wanted me to handle it from there, but she said she would continue to do it.

She replied to the outlet, and they had some additional questions about frequency and ad placement. She emailed me to ask for some help on those. I provided some advice and she continued on.

The media outlet provided her with an ad, and she sent it to me for my opinion. There were some errors in the ad, and the best marketing points were not mentioned. I told her what I thought she should do and offered to redo the ad for her. She opted to have the media outlet fix it because they didn't charge to do that. She communicated back to the advertising rep.

They sent a second ad proof, and she forwarded it to me. Two of the changes we wanted had not been made, so I pointed those out. She replied to the rep for a third proof. By this time, it was too late to make the deadline for that week's edition, so they rescheduled the ad for the following week.

The person she had been dealing with was on holidays the following week, so the new advertising rep followed up with wanting to know where she stood on the advertising. She reviewed the discussion with them, and after two more emails, she finally got the ad finalized for publication.

I reviewed this process with the client, and noted that she had spent fifteen hours communicating with the advertising rep and myself! My bill was for 1.5 hours of time to email back and forth with her and explain the advertising. Spending fifteen hours communicating had forced her to work on Sunday to catch up on some of the time she had missed doing all the emailing. In addition, she had missed the deadline for the advertising and had to wait a week, which caused her to have to change her promotional efforts timeline.

Had I handled all the communications for her, and designed the ad, it would have been an extra hour of time on my end, and only an hour of her time in total. The deadline would have been met, her promotion would have happened on time and she would not have had to work Sunday to make up for the missed time in her business.

After we reviewed that experience together, she saw how she needed to make better decisions about her time if she was to grow her business effectively. Being financially conscientious was important to her, as it is to all of us, but she was learning that there were also costs to being inefficient. The fifteen hours she spent on the advertising placement earned her no money and cost her extra working hours to compensate for that missed time. While she worked a weekend to catch up, what if she didn't have that luxury the next time?

While every business owner is responsible for all aspects of the business, you don't have to do everything yourself. Find experts to help you.

"Until we can manage time, we can manage nothing else."–Peter Drucker, Management Consultant

20

Making a Budget for Marketing

Regardless of the size of your business, you should have a budget for marketing. It acts as a guide to help you manage your finances in a way that contributes to growing your business.

To make a relevant budget for marketing, you need to know a) what do you want to do and b) how much it will cost to do those things. The next chapter takes you through developing a one-page marketing plan which may be of assistance to you in coming up with a budget. If you regularly budget for marketing, you will have history to reference as well. Here are some considerations for items to include in your budget:

Who Will Do the Work?

You can do the marketing work yourself, contract it out to a marketing agency, or have a combination of insourcing and outsourcing duties. When doing the work yourself, ensure you have the time to prioritize marketing, the expertise to do it well, and the capability of following through on the commitment. You can refer to the chapter on insourcing and outsourcing for tips on making these decisions.

What Support Materials Will You Need?

Two considerations accompany this answer: improving the materials you already have and adding new materials you will need.

Improving Current Materials

It is a good idea to review your website at least once a year so the content remains a current reflection of your business. Your website is a key marketing tool and you may decide to make some additions or deletions to support your marketing plan initiatives. The same holds true for printed materials you make available to customers, promotional banners, signage you use at events, tradeshow giveaways you have on hand, and advertising you have pre-purchased that runs into the new marketing year. Keep what works, change what needs changing, and replace anything out of date.

Adding New Materials

If you have decided to become an event sponsor, you may benefit from adding a portable banner or logoed tent that you can take to events. If you are launching a new product, you may want to contract marketing services to help make that launch successful and sustainable. If you plan to be more active on social media, you may choose to invest in some advertising that drives people to your page.

One of the ways to keep people engaged is by a regular email communication. Email is a money saver in that you don't incur printing costs, and it can be more efficient at sending out news in a timely fashion. Adding an email communication strategy to your marketing involves two key points:

- You must have a regular publishing schedule
- You must publish something that the reader will find helpful and interesting

Think of your email communication as a customer newsletter. You might provide some tips that help customers, interesting facts, beneficial news (i.e.: legislation changes), updates from your business (i.e.: new hires or new products, awards, upcoming event participation, etc.), and something lighthearted, such as highlighting National Hamburger Day or National Nurses Week or something like that. When people find your email interesting, they will continue to want to receive it, and new people will want to subscribe to it.

The benefit to a regular email communication is you can use it to support other marketing initiatives. You can print copies of your newsletter to distribute in-store, at events, or provide to current or new customers. When you can reuse marketing materials for different initiatives in your marketing plan, you get better value for your marketing spend.

Evaluating the Value

As you look at some of the costs of your marketing initiatives, be careful of drawing comparisons. Instead of looking at a $1,000 event sponsorship for one day versus $1,000 in social media advertising for a month, look at what each opportunity offers you and consider the value.

The $1,000 event sponsorship might be one day, but it comes with several acknowledgements throughout the media, including social media. You can also share this event on your social media pages leading up to the event, the day of the event, and after the event has ended. Your sponsorship may also allow you to be on site and meet people face-to-face or to be connected to a cause that has a lot of community support.

The $1,000 in social media ads can last thirty days and drive people to your page or website. From there, the goal is for them to read your social media posts and form a positive impression of your business or visit your website and find some information that prompts them to contact you. Like all advertising, it is less personal but targets a mass audience.

The $1,000 in the examples above provides different benefits to the business, so it's not as easy as comparing the cost alone. You need to reach different people in different ways, and having a variety of marketing initiatives that work together in promoting your business is the best way to grow your brand.

Some Final Notes

As you allocate money to each of your planned marketing initiatives, you may notice you are exceeding your budget or coming in under budget. Before you cancel or add an initiative to your plan, consider ways to maintain the initiative by changing the marketing commitment. Here are some examples of how you can do that:

- Reduce a four-page brochure to a one-page flyer (saves on printing but still provides a key marketing piece)
- Instead of ordering promotional giveaways for a tradeshow event, purchase something from a local business to use as a raffle
- If a sponsorship opportunity allows, ask to be on site at the event and provide an extra item for participants
- Talk to your advertising sales rep and ask for an ad package that fits the new budget
- Prioritize promotional spend to the target audience who is most likely to yield you results or add promotional spend to a potential new target audience
- Substitute your product or service for dollars; a caterer could contribute some charcuterie boards for an event instead of a $500 sponsorship
- Instead of buying wine to serve at your open house, ask a local winery to provide a tasting

With every completed initiative, make some notes so you can improve on your initiative for next year, such as what worked well and what didn't work as well as you had hoped. This feedback can help you make the best impressions for your customers and keep your bottom line moving forward.

Download at template of a marketing budget for free!

www.forwardthinkingbook.com

21

The One-Page Marketing Plan

Making decisions about marketing, advertising and promotions is easier to do if you have a marketing plan for your business. If the term '*marketing plan*' makes you feel a bit overwhelmed, don't worry; you can get a great start with just one page. In your business, you know the easier you can make it for a customer to buy from you, the more successful you will be. The same is true for managing your marketing. The easier you make it for yourself, the more successful your marketing decisions will be. Here's an example of how to create a one-year marketing guide on one page.

On a sheet of paper, make a chart three rows across and four rows down. This will give you twelve boxes—one for each month. Label each box with a month, moving left to right, with January, February, and March across the top. This has the added benefit of ending each row in a quarter. See below:

ABC Law Corporation

January	February	March
April	May	June
July	August	September
October	November	December

Note any important marketing opportunities throughout the year. These could include an annual customer appreciation day, business anniversary, special event promotion time (i.e.: Mother's Day, Nurses Month), tendering times, annual charitable events, etc. Note everything that provides an opportunity for your business, including not only what your commitments are currently, but also other opportunities you might have.

Your one-pager now looks something like this: ABC Law Corporation

January	February	March
Wills and estate planning (health directives)	Wills and estate planning Valentine's Day (weddings) Local winter festival	Wills and estate planning Real estate International Women's Day
April	**May**	**June**
Wills and estate planning Real estate Easter (family gathering)	Real estate (cottage) Business anniversary	Real estate

July	August	September
Real estate	Real estate Realtor's golf tournament	Real estate Wills and estates (tax planning)
October Wills and estates (powers of attorney) Thanksgiving (family gathering)	**November** Wills and estates (planned giving, trusts)	**December** Wills and estates Christmas (family gathering) Realtor's Christmas event

Once you have everything on your page, your next step is to make the list of marketing work you will need to do. This may include updates to current materials (website, brochure, etc.), registration for events, social media post ideas, and more. Put every idea you have on this list.

Note: It can be helpful to work backwards from the events set in the calendar to organize what you need to do in advance.

In the example below, January is when an update to the website is made to include newlywed legal information, as talking to newlyweds can happen in February and March with a link to the website for more information.

For ABC Law Corporation, the first three months of their calendar might look like this:

January	February	March
Wills/estate planning (health)	Wills and estate planning Valentine's Day Local winter festival	Wills/estate planning Real estate International Women's Day
• *Update website to have a page for 'newly married'* • *Plan participation in local winter festival* • *Social media posts on power of attorney (health), newlywed legal matters, talking about will and estate planning with family and promo of local winter festival participation*	• *Register for International Women's Day event* • *Social media posts on local festival draw winner, newlyweds' legal matters, will and estate planning (choosing an executor), preview of International Women's Day*	• *Attend International Women's Day event* • *Send out invitations for business anniversary wine and cheese* • *Send a letter to local realtors with list of services* • *Social media posts on International Women's Day event, making a will together for the first time, what to expect from real estate legal services, how to talk about estate planning with family*

The Final Step

Now you can see the time commitment you must invest to do everything on your list, and you may find it is not reasonable to do all of it. For example, March is a busy month with will and estate planning work, the kick-off to real estate legal work season, invites to the business anniversary wine and cheese, attending the International Women's Day event, and making all the social media posts. This is where you make revisions so your marketing plan is something you can comfortably do while also doing the business work.

The final version of the first three months of ABC Law Corporation looks like this:

January Wills/estate planning (health)	February Wills and estate planning Valentine's Day Local winter festival	March Wills/estate planning Real estate International Women's Day
• *Update website to have a page for 'newly married'* • *Plan participation in local winter festival* • *Social media posts on power of attorney (health), newlywed legal matters, talking about will and estate planning with family and promo of local winter festival participation*	• *Register for International Women's Day event* • *Social media posts on local festival draw winner, newlyweds' legal matters, will and estate planning (choosing an executor), preview of International Women's Day* • *Hire someone to do business anniversary wine and cheese with invites to key contacts and local realtors*	• *Attend International Women's Day event* • *Social media posts on International Women's Day event, making a will together for the first time, what to expect from real estate legal services, how to talk about estate planning with family*

ABC Law Corporation decided to outsource the planning for the business anniversary event so someone else could manage all that work. The initially planned letter campaign to realtors to inform them of ABC Law Corporation services was deleted, and the realtors were included in the business anniversary invitations, still connecting to them but not incurring an additional time-consuming marketing element.

The Benefits of the One-Page Marketing Plan

Your marketing plan is an overview for the year, and it will fit on one page. You can use the back of the page to make any more detailed notes.

Once you have your one-year marketing plan, when someone approaches you for advertising or event sponsorship, you can see your commitments on one page and evaluate if the request will work for what you want to accomplish. If a new opportunity arises, you can more easily determine if it can reasonably fit into your schedule based on what you have planned or if you are willing to replace it with something you already had planned.

Once you have this template in place, it becomes easier to use every year as you simply add and delete items to your calendar.

What About the Cost?

The cost of fulfilling your marketing plan is not absent by mistake. Marketing is something you must do to sustain and grow your business, so planning what initiatives will enable you to do that is the entire focus of creating the one-pager. In the next chapter, the focus is on the marketing budget and what you will be comfortable allocating to these initiatives. If finances are tight, you will adjust what you are willing to spend. If time is tight, you will adjust how you will get things done. The lead thinking in marketing is always to accomplish the initiative, whether it happens exactly as you had imagined it would or with some deviation.

You can only benefit from the marketing if you do the marketing.

Download the One Page Marketing Plan template for free.

www.forwardthinkingbook.com

22

Insource or Outsource Your Marketing

Most small businesses will not have an employee who has the sole job of marketing. Usually, marketing is the responsibility of the business owner, and often, the marketing work is outsourced. As the business grows, the owner may delegate some marketing aspects to employees who are also filling other roles in the company, and a combination of insourcing and outsourcing of marketing work takes place. Even when the business grows to accommodate a dedicated marketing position, there can still be a choice to outsource marketing work.

When deciding when to complete marketing work internally (insource) or hire a contracted agency to help (outsource), here are some tips to help you make the best choice:

Where Do You Want to Focus?

A key advantage of outsourcing your marketing work is you can focus on other aspects of the business where you have the expertise. As the owner, you might be working on forming relationships, attending events, building the profile of the company, or even being hands-on in the work of the business. The contracted marketing agency creates the strategy, writes the copy, designs the artwork, meets with sales and sponsorship reps, and handles all that detail work. You approve the end result, but you don't have to spend your time in the weeds, putting it all together.

When you insource your marketing work, you will still maintain more involvement in marketing, but some of the work will become another person's responsibility. There may be elements of the marketing work that still need to be contracted out, because the employee (or the owner) may not have all the skills required to do it. When marketing stays in house, it becomes a task that needs to be managed, and that takes a time commitment.

Evaluating the Cost

When you outsource marketing, you are paying for someone's time to do this work. However, for that cost, you are also getting the infrastructure that comes with a professional agency or consultant. This includes someone who is educated and experienced in marketing—a specialist in the field. They have ideas, and they know what makes a good strategy. They know how to handle sales reps and what makes advertising work most effectively. They are negotiators and opportunity seekers. Professional marketers can also access information more quickly because they know their industry. It is important to note that marketing is not a one-off task; to be effective, you need to make a long-term commitment, and you should consider that in the cost evaluation.

Taking on the marketing work internally will require you to build your own infrastructure and evaluate what you can do yourself and what you need help to accomplish. Instead of hiring an agency, you may only need to hire a graphic designer or a web designer. While you will need to research the best options for the task, once you have made a decision, you must build this piece of infrastructure.

The important factor here is that the internal person who is managing the marketing responsibility has the time and expertise to get it accomplished effectively. If marketing is one part of their work, you need to provide direction on how they will prioritize their varying responsibilities. Your costs could be less, as the time element will be covered under the employee's salary, but you will likely have some outside costs as well with select expertise. You should also factor in the cost of the employee's time to do the marketing work as a comparison to what it might cost to outsource the work. For example, if an employee who earns $25 an hour is tasked with ten hours a week of marketing, that's $250 a week or $1,000 a month. What kind of time does that buy you with an agency?

Recognizing the Skillsets

You built your business on a set of skills that solve a problem for your customer. There have likely been times when you needed to contract out to another business to complete a project because they had a certain skillset you needed and which you didn't have to complete the project. The same happens in marketing.

Seasoned marketing professionals are experts in what they do. Like you, they have a certain set of highly developed skills in this field. (Don't be afraid to ask for the qualifications or resume of the outsourced company you are thinking of hiring.) Your decision on outsourcing is whether you need those skills or if you can still achieve your marketing goals on your own or by investing in some education or training to do them yourself.

When you do the work internally, you may not get the same results you would with a professional marketer, but you may get results good enough to keep you moving forward. If you have always done your work internally, you may choose to invest in professional services to see the difference, then you can more easily decide if outsourcing is a beneficial contributor to your business or if you can manage without it.

Sometimes good enough is good enough. Sometimes you need the very best result possible. Assess your expectations for your marketing to help you choose where outsourcing or insourcing will most benefit your business.

Handling the Control Factor

For some owners, the critical factor in insourcing or outsourcing marketing work will be how much they are willing to let someone else participate in their business. I have had discussions with many business owners who didn't have time (or expertise) to do their marketing work, but they still weren't ready to let someone else in on the operation of their business. You must decide what matters more: having complete control over the marketing process or getting the marketing done well.

When you outsource marketing work, you must share your business goals with someone so they know how to best position you to achieve those goals. It might be that you want to increase revenue by a certain amount, break into a new territory, challenge a competitor, or add a new type of client. You need to be comfortable with someone else knowing this information and working on your behalf to make it happen. Professional agencies and consultants usually have confidentiality agreements or understandings so they won't share your discussions with a competitor, but you should always ask for that if you have concerns.

When you insource marketing, all that information is kept internally. However, if employees leave, they take that knowledge with them to someone else, and no protection is in place for that. When you hire an employee, you get their knowledge and skills, and that holds true for an employee who leaves your business to work for someone else. However, marketing strategies are specific to a certain business and don't easily transfer to a competitor because operations will differ.

The bottom line is that you can't do everything yourself if you want to grow your business. You must trust people with different aspects of your business, so the decision you have to make is where marketing falls on that list.

Final Thoughts

Hiring outside help for marketing is not required for any business. It is a tool that can help you grow your business if you don't have the time to commit to marketing or the expertise to know what will bring you the best return on your investment. The best marketing results will come with a consistent and sustainable effort, so be prepared to make that commitment whether you outsource or insource or opt for a combination of both options.

23

How to Handle the Critics

If there are two things you can count on when you operate a business, it is that there will always be competitors, and there will always be critics. This chapter is about the critics.

Thanks to social media, more and more people are freely taking on the role of critic from behind the protection of their screens. In many cases, if you are an ethical and professional business, much of that criticism will likely take care of itself without you expending much effort. Others may come to your rescue, or it will become evident that those doing the criticizing are just looking for attention.

I remember when a chamber of commerce held their annual awards gala and posted some photos of the event the following week. Several people commented positively, but one person posted criticism about the event operation. Several others came to the chamber's rescue with answers to the critic, and the chamber director didn't have to say anything. The critic eventually apologized for the comment and commended the chamber on a successful event.

In other cases, you might need a strategy to handle the criticism. In my line of work, I handle critics a lot, because I am usually proposing new ideas or changes to a business or organization in order for them to achieve at a higher level. Change is something most people are not comfortable with, and it tends to draw out critics. It's not so much that they are against the idea, it's just they are uncomfortable with change, or they have a competing agenda. Regardless of the motivation behind the criticism, your job is to have a strategy to deal with it. Your goal is not to change the critics but to hold course despite them.

I solved this problem in my business by going to a counsellor for some advice.

An organization had hired me on a marketing contract— something they had never done before. However, as they were desperate to build awareness, they decided to hire some expertise. Some members of the organization felt marketing was not a useful expense and consistently argued against any suggestion I brought forward. Although I explained the rationale, I quickly found they were not looking to learn more about the opportunities I presented; they were looking to not spend money on marketing, period. I learned, over time, other agendas were at play that caused this disruption, but I had hoped our achievements would help to bring them on board with how marketing assists in reaching their organization's goals. Unfortunately, that wasn't what they wanted. I reached the point of either resigning from the contract or finding a strategy to handle the critics. This is when I went to the counsellor.

The counsellor referred me to a YouTube video by a social worker/researcher, Brené Brown. It's twenty-two minutes long and worth the watch[9]:

Brown shared how she encountered critics as her professional profile grew, and it led her to a famous speech by Theodore Roosevelt, often referred to as The Man in the Arena. The part of the speech she referenced went like this:

It is not the critic who counts; not the man who points out how the strong man stumbles, or where the doer of deeds could have done them better. The credit belongs to the man who is actually in the arena, whose face is marred by dust and sweat and blood; who at the best knows in the end the triumph of high achievement, and who at the worst, if he fails, at least fails while daring greatly.

Brown talked about the decision you make to be '*in the arena*' and show up for something, much like a business owner shows up for their proposal or recommendation. She talked about what happens when you make that decision.

"*If you're going to show up and be seen, you're going to get your ass kicked. That's a guarantee. If you're going to go in the arena and spend any time in there, you will get*

[9]https://www.youtube.com/watch?v=8-JXOnFOXQk&t=1002s

your ass kicked." From this, she developed her own philosophy on criticism: *"If you're not in the arena also getting your ass kicked, I'm not interested in your feedback."*

She finished her talk by saying she no longer tries to avoid the critics but, instead, expects them to show up and actually creates a place for them, saying, *"I see you, I hear you, but I'm going to show up and do this anyway. And I've got a seat for you, and you're welcome to come, but I'm not interested in your feedback."*

I have watched that video close to one hundred times. I have shared it with everyone I know who faces a challenge with critics. In my own situation referenced earlier, I made a new strategy at the committee when it came to marketing.

When one of the members levied a criticism, I thanked them for their concern and would keep an eye on it as we moved forward. I kept repeating that line with every criticism brought forward. That acknowledgement resulted in fewer disruptions in the meetings, and after a while, they stopped criticizing.

As a business owner, you can operate without being *'in the arena.'* However, if you choose to be more public with your business, something that can result from good marketing, more courageous bidding, or moving into a larger storefront, there will be critics. Expect them, welcome them, but remind yourself that you are not interested in their feedback. Then keep on taking your business to the next level.

24

Recognize Your Small Business Strengths

Part of my career has been working with small businesses and organizations in small communities. Organization Many smaller enterprises feel they are disadvantaged by not having the resources available at larger organizations, so they default to low expectations of what they could realistically accomplish with marketing. However, small businesses often don't see their own strengths when it comes to growing their business, and there are many.

Flexibility

Small businesses have significantly more flexibility in their marketing options than larger businesses that are often confined to certain ways of doing things, because that is what they can do on a larger scale. Larger organizations often use a one-size-fits-all approach, because they are making the marketing decision on that larger scale. For example, large retail businesses use flyers to reach people, because they can do that in every market where they are located. This leaves the local niche market open to small businesses where customers can be treated more individually.

When I started a local health magazine, I sent the information to small and large organizations alike. I never had interest from large organizations, because I was a regional publication, and the media they focused on was national. This gave me a very strong marketing pitch for smaller businesses and organizations to be in a publication that the big players didn't want any part of. We had a professional product that focused on local information, and people truly loved it. It was an opportunity for small organizations to speak directly to the people they needed to reach, and could do it because they were flexible enough to adjust their marketing efforts to include this publication.

Shorter Path to the Decision Maker

In small businesses, it is not uncommon to deal directly with the decision maker. In large organizations, you usually have a few levels to get through before you find the person who can make the decision. Having a shorter path to the person you need to talk with makes for a more efficient conversation or transaction. For customers, not having to be on hold with a 1–800 number saves time, and time is something for which we all have a limited supply.

In providing some marketing work for a small business, I heard that one of the expenses they wanted to review was the annual fees to a company that managed their website.

They had done their own research and felt they could just pay for the website hosting directly and save themselves a few hundred dollars in fees that the website provider was charging. I asked them to explain their process for making website changes. The business said they would call a certain person at the website company to make their changes. The person did so fairly quickly and charged a fee for that service. For a business that made changes monthly, that direct process was efficient.

As we were meeting, I suggested we call the website hosting company to see what their process would be. We dialed the 1-800 number and went through the prompts to get to the right department. They told us the wait would be about twenty minutes, but they could call us back if we wanted. The business owner chose that option. We continued with our meeting, and at the twenty minute mark, the phone rang with an automated message from the website host. We again followed the prompts and got to a representative. The representative referred us to a page on the website that explained their processes, but there was one element of the client's website that wasn't included there. The representative said he would ask his supervisor and placed us on a brief hold. When he returned, he referred us to another page on the website. The client thanked him for his time and hung up the phone. *"I'm not going through that every month for a few hundred bucks,"* he said. And we moved on to evaluate other expenses.

Relationships

It can be challenging to build relationships with big businesses. The bigger the organization, usually the more demands there are on the leaders' time. When you deal with small businesses, you have a greater opportunity to build a relationship, and many times, that will likely be with the decision maker.

A client of mine wanted to purchase a piece of equipment that would help them be more efficient in their business. They searched online as to where they could get the equipment and contacted several large, non-local companies. The equipment was on backorder with everyone they called, so they decided to just get on a list and wait.

In one of our marketing discussions, they mentioned the issue, and I suggested that maybe someone locally could help them. They felt fairly certain the equipment was too customized to be done locally but thanked me for my suggestion. Four months later, they called to take me up on the offer.

Later that day, I called one of my other clients who dealt in the industry, and he referred me to another local business and said, "*Use my name when you call him.*" That morning, I forwarded the information to my client who needed the equipment. The next day, he emailed me to say the business had been to their location and had provided them with a quote, which they had accepted. He could not believe how fast that happened. The equipment was custom built to their needs and installed within two weeks, which allowed the business to increase output at the start of the busiest season.

Building relationships is one of the best financial decisions you will make in your business. Knowing who to go to for the things you need will not only save you time, but also make others aware of your business so they can refer you when someone asks them for help.

Capitalizing On Opportunity

In larger businesses and organizations, the focus on marketing is on the majority. These organizations do a lot of research on what appeals to the most people, and their marketing efforts reflect that. You can learn a lot about what audiences the larger businesses are *not* targeting by paying attention to the audiences they *are* targeting.

An easy example of this is large food retail. Large retail stores promote almost entirely on price. They are reaching the audience who cares more about price than anything when it comes to groceries. Yet there are small business food stores in so many communities. How on earth are they surviving? By capitalizing on an opportunity too small for big business but perfect for them.

Delis and speciality food stores market on things like quality, uniqueness, and food knowledge to seize an opportunity. Their customers are those who want a higher-end type of food to celebrate a special occasion, as a treat, or even on a regular basis. They might patronize this local deli occasionally or as a regular part of their grocery shopping.

While they can get steak at a food chain store, they want the freshly butchered steak from the deli. While they can get buns at the food chain store, they want the homemade ones from the local bakery.

The small business doesn't need to make the same amount of money that a large food chain store needs to make to be viable. Because of this flexibility, they have more opportunities to capture niche market customers and build something sustainable and profitable. The marketing the big food stores do in flyers and advertising doesn't even impact the small business food store, because they aren't in a grocery price war.

As a small business, you exist with larger businesses—on your street, in the town next door, and online. However, their marketing efforts are not your marketing efforts. Lead with your strengths and let the big businesses battle it out amongst themselves. They are not your competition.

About the Author

After being turned down for more than 80 communications roles because she was "over-qualified" for the position, Jennifer launched Forward Thinking Marketing Agency in her hometown of Pembroke, Ontario, and began life as a small business owner.

Jennifer came to open the business after spending several years as a professional golfer on the Canadian women's golf circuit. Creating her own business allowed her to combine her two strengths–communications expertise and fierce competitiveness–and put her efforts toward helping other small businesses and organizations reach their full potential. Jennifer has consulted with hundreds of clients in sectors such as insurance, social services, aerospace, property development, community building, healthcare, agriculture, retail, and professional services. She is also on the digital marketing team for a U.S.-based, franchise-focused marketing agency.

A graduate of Campbell University, where she earned her degree in Mass Communications and the title of Big South Conference Player of the Year in college golf, Jennifer spends her time between her home province of Ontario, Canada, and her college state of North Carolina. She is a member of the National Speaker's Association and has a lifelong commitment to professional development including the Proctor Gallagher Institute Thinking Into Results training which prompted the writing of this book.

Forward Thinking for Your Business is Jennifer's first book.

Follow Jennifer at:

 www.forwardthinkingbook.com